from Wade + Audrey

Christmas 1987

青い鳥をさがして

In Search of
MOUNTAIN BLUEBIRDS

Photographed by GALEN BURRELL

グラフィック社

Photographed by Galen Burrell
Text by Ron Hirschi
Translation by Hajime Komanoya

In Search of MOUNTAIN BLUEBIRDS
Copyright © 1987 Graphic-sha Publishing Co., Ltd.
1-9-12, Kudan-kita, Chiyoda-ku, Tokyo 102 Japan
ISBN 4-7661-0427-7

Printed in Japan
First Printing, April 1987

目 次 CONTENTS

ギャレン・バレルと共に歩いて

ロン・ハーシュ
エッセイスト

もし，ギャレン・バレルや彼の撮った北アメリカの鳥たちの美しく繊細な写真について，もっとよく知りたいというのでしたら，あなたはまず彼とそのテーマである鳥たちを探しに出かけて行かなくてはなりません。アスペンの木立のはずれから淡紅色に芽ぶいた柳の立ち並ぶ小川に沿って，木々の続くはるか高みへと出向いてみます。するとどうでしょう。いつのまにかあなたは，ロッキー山脈の春の静けさの中に舞うブルーバードの一群れを追いかけているのです。私は，ギャレンと共に，何度となく旅をしてきました。共に道を辿りながらいつも思うのは，道という道が全てこうしたロッキー山脈のような静かな場所に続いているという事実です。しかも，それぞれ独持の落ち着いた美しさをそなえているのです。さらに奥深く進んで行くうちに，私たちは動物たちとの穏やかな心の触れ合いのようなものを感じ始めます。そして，いつのまにか私たちをすっかり取り囲んでいる彼らの気配に触れる時，私にはギャレン・バレルが，本当に動物たちのことばを話せるように思えてくるのです。

彼には特別な才能があります。動物たちを非常によく知っているのです。このような知識があるからこそ，彼らの素顔をいきいきと捉えることに成功しているのでしょう。彼の撮影技術に対する人々の関心も高まってきています。しかしながら，ギャレンはきまっていうのです。「もっと動物そのものに関心を持って欲しい。僕個人のことや，写真がきれいかどうかなどということから目をそらして……」と。

ページをめくってみますと，まるで開け放たれた窓からアメリカの風景が見えるようです。同時に，その風景が連続していく様子は，この多様な国を行き来する旅のひとつのあり方を語っているようです。つまり，ギャレン・バレルの後を追いつつ，ふるさとの心を探し求める旅でもあるのです。

旅への道は海辺から始まっています。森をさ迷い，農地や平原，砂漠を横切って進みます。湿原地，乾燥地をぬい，名も知らぬ川の流れに沿って，いつしか写真は西部に連なる高峰に私たちを導きます。

そして下って行きます。まるでブルーバードの翼に乗っているかのように……。

それぞれの風景の中で，ギャレンは多くの鳥たちを紹介してくれます。彼は常にひとつの独立した対象として鳥を見つめるようにしています。その鳥たちを眺めれば，どこを訪れたかもよくわかるようになっているのです。優雅な表情が次々と映し出されていきます。薄紅の装いをしたヘラサギ。カナダガン。さらに，黄金色（こがねいろ）のフウキンチョウがアメリカに生きる心優しい住人として，歓迎のまなざしを送ってくれます。

私たちの世界に取りつけられたこれらの窓の数々からは，また多くの点で意義深いものが示されています。たとえ現実の自然が荒れ果てて移り変わっても，私たちはこれらの窓から眺めることによって，心の中に何らかの希望を持てるような気さえしてくるのです。

この道を辿りながらアメリカを横断する時，あなたは鳥たちの目の中に宿るある種の明るさを感じるでしょう。鳥たちは今もなお自然の中に調和しながら生きています。その彼らの生活の見事な美しさが，考えに考え抜かれた刻限の中で捉えられています。もうまもなく終わろうとしている冬のある朝，ブルーバードの群れが上空から舞い降りてきます。まるではるか彼方に過ぎ去った夏空の小さな切れ端のようにやってきます。その柔らかな青い羽毛が，冷気に満ちた静けさの中でふわりふわりと脹んでいきます。じっと見つめる彼らのまなざしは，私たちの想念を貫くようにも思えます。カメラのシャッターがカチリと音をたて，一陣の冷たい風がヒューと吹いて川の流れのように通り抜けていくと，突然，鳥たちは空へ舞い上り，消え去ります。ああ，彼らの後を追って飛ぶことができたら…。不意にこみあげる憧れのようなものを抱きながら，私たちはじっと立ちつくしてしまいます。けれども，その後には，再び小道が幾条（いくすじ）も続いています。そう，これからも春は幾度となくめぐってくるのです……。

INTRODUCTION

by Ron Hirschi
Essayist

If you are curious to know more about Galen Burrell and his delicate photographs of North American birds, you must search for him and his subjects at the edge of aspen groves, along streams lined with pink-stemmed willows, or high above the line of trees where you might follow a flock of bluebirds in the serenity of a Rocky Mountain spring.....

I have traveled with Galen many times and retracing those paths, I know they all lead to these kinds of quiet places, each with its own peaceful beauty. They also lead to a gentle understanding of animals—animals that surround us all, and animals that Galen Burrell seems truly able to speak with in their own language.

His is a special gift—to know animals so well. With that knowledge has come success in portraying animals in their homes and much interest in his photographic skills. Yet, he would ask that we be most curious about the animals themselves, turning away from questions about himself or, even, about his exquisite photographs.

Look through these pages as if they were open windows on American landscapes. Together, the view comprises a journey across this diverse country, a journey that follows Galen Burrell's search for the heart of this land. The path begins on the ocean shore, wandering through forests, crossing farmland, prairie, and desert. Through wet marsh, dry sagelands, and along unnamed streams, the photos eventually lead us up high mountains of the west, then down, as if on the wings of a bluebird.

In each landscape, Burrell introduces us to many kinds of birds, always offering a view of the bird as an individual as well as a fitting example of the residents of each special place visited. All the while, these elegant impressions of pink-feathered spoonbills, Canada geese, and golden tanagers provide a welcome glimpse of the gentlest inhabitants of America.

In many ways, these windows on our world offer something far greater too; they offer hope for a land that has seen so many harsh changes.

While following this pathway across America, you will see a bright promise in the eyes of birds that still live in harmony with the land. The majestic beauty of their existence is captured in many thoughtful moments, beginning on a late winter morning when a flock of mountain bluebirds descends from above like tiny pieces of a distant summer sky. Their soft, blue feathers fluff in the cold stillness. Their gaze seems to penetrate our thoughts as a camera shutter clicks and a cold breeze rushes past like an icy river. Then, suddenly the birds leap skyward and vanish.

If we could only follow their flight, holding the wonder of that moment forever. But, then, there are so many paths to follow, so many springs to come.....

旅に寄せて

ギャレン・バレル

この写真集は、海辺から山の頂きまで続く、1本の道を旅するという想定で構成されている。そしてこの道は、ジョージア、フロリダ、ルイジアナ州の沿岸部湿地帯から始まっているのである。

高地へと登り進むうちに、森や農場を通り抜けていく。そこは、人々が依然として野生の動物たちと自然を共有している場所でもある。さらに高みへと進む。西へと、奥深く分け入っていく。大平原の面影がロッキー山脈の東面に沿ってのこされている。ここが次の舞台である。この章の砂漠の写真には、南へ下って撮ったもの、あるいはロッキー山脈南端のさらに向こう側にあるアリゾナ州サハロ・ナショナルモニュメントや、テキサス中南部のチワワン砂漠で撮ったものなども含まれている。

「ウィロークリーク」の写真は、澄みきった川に沿いながら、何度となく旅した時のものである。その清らかな水は、ロッキー山脈から流れ落ちて、モンタナ、ワイオミング、コロラド州を通り抜けている。沼地の写真はロッキー山脈のふもとで撮影したものである。ロッキーの山並みはこうした「柳の立ち並ぶ小川」のふるさとでもある。

山間部の写真は、大部分ロッキー山脈の中で撮影した。マウンテンブルーバードの故郷、そしてそのはずれから西部は始まっている…。

THE JOURNEY — An Explanation of Photo Sequence

GALEN BURRELL

The sequence of photos follows a path from the ocean's edge to the mountain tops, beginning in coastal swamps of the Georgia, Florida, and Louisiana lowlands.

Climbing to higher ground, this photographic journey leads through forest and farmlands in which people still share their land with wild animals. Higher still, and farther to the west, the remnants of shortgrass prairie along the eastern face of the Rocky Mountains is the setting for the next photo grouping. The desert photos in this sequence are from farther to the south and beyond the southern tip of the Rockies within the Saguaro National Monument of Arizona and the Chihuahuan Desert of South Central Texas.

The willow creek photos represent many trips along the clear streams flowing down from the Rocky Mountains of Montana, Wyoming, and Colorado and the majority of the marsh images were taken at the base of the mountains where these willow creeks were born.

With few exceptions, the mountain photographs were taken within the Rocky Mountains, home of the mountain bluebird and at the edge of where the west begins.....

Galen Burrell

海鳴りが間近に迫るとはいえ、ここ湿地帯は静かなものだ。ボボリンクやヨシゴイが、細い茎の上に止まっている。一羽のサギが魚の群れに忍び寄り、ピンクの羽毛をしたヘラサギが、ぬかるみから身を起こす。やがて、掘り起こされた土が、打ち寄せる波に洗い流されてゆく。突然、翼のはばたく音が頭上に聞こえたかと思うと、シラサギの群れが見える。そのはばたきに導かれて進んでゆくうちに、沼の神秘な声が自身の身の上を語りかけてくる。その時、あなたは気づくはずである。この湿潤な世界には生命が溢れていると。
ここアメリカ南東部の海に沿いながら、旅は始まる。
この章では、もっと離れた地域の写真も何枚か載っている。たとえば、鉤爪を開いたワシの写真は、大陸の反対部分、太平洋側の北西部で撮ったものである。ルイジアナやジョージアの湿地帯の鳥たちと同様に、ワシが巣を作る場所というのは、大陸が海と接するところなのである。彼らはサケを求めてピュージェット・サウンドの湾岸を飛んでいる。
いくつかの美しい沼や塩沢をあげてみると、アメリカには次のようなものがある。サバンナ国立野性生物保護区（ジョージア）、サビーン国立野性生物保護区（ルイジアナ）。その他数多くの湿地帯が、フロリダやテキサス湾岸沿いにある。同様に、太平洋沿岸の美しい沼地は、ワシントン、オレゴン、カリフォルニアなどに点在している。

The coastal swamp is silent though it is so near the ocean's roar. Bobolinks and bitterns stand on slender stems. A heron stalks schools of fish and pink-feathered spoonbills rise from soft mud that will soon be washed into the pounding surf. Then, you hear the sound of wings overhead—a flock of egrets. And, the sound seems to lead you on until the mysterious voices of the swamp reveal themselves more fully and you see that life abounds in this wet world.

Here, along the southeastern coast of America, this journey begins.

There are also photos in this segment of more distant places; the eagle with talons spread was photographed at the opposite end of the continent in the Pacific Northwest. Like the Louisiana and Georgia swamp birds, the eagle is at home where land meets the sea. You can watch them as they search for salmon along the shores of Puget Sound.

Some of the most beautiful swamps and salt marshes in America include the Savannah National Wildlife Refuge in Georgia, Sabine National Wildlife Refuge in Louisiana, and the numerous wetlands in Florida and along the Gulf coast of Texas, as well as the Pacific coastal marshes of Washington, Oregon and California.

海辺の湿地帯より
COASTAL SWAMP

海辺の湿地帯より
COASTAL SWAMP

カワセミ：Kingfisher

どんよりと曇った日。カワセミが小魚を探して流木の上にとまっている。フロリダのオレンジ畑や、マングローブの沼など、アメリカではどこにでも見られる鳥である。(ワシントン)

シラサギの群れ：A gathering of egrets

早春のある日。サバンナリバーの近くでは、潮のひくころあいを見計らって、ダイサギやユキコサギ、コウノトリ、トキたちが、餌をついばんでいた。小さな群れを作って仲間と一緒にいることの多い彼らが、こんな風に集まっているのは珍しい。（ジョージア）

ベニヘラサギ：Roseate spoonbills

雨の春の朝。ベニヘラサギのピンクの羽が、鉛色の空によく映える。外気は冷たく、また長い間ひとつの場所に立っていたために、手がかじかんでしまった。かろうじて、シャッターを押したことを覚えている。（ルイジアナ）

コヨシゴイ：Bittern on slender stems

よく晴れた春の日。朝の早い時間から、コヨシゴイを眺められるのは嬉しいものである。そ
れにしても、沼の植物の中にいる彼等を見つけ出すのは、なかなか難しい。（ジョージア）

ボボリンク：Bobolink

はるか北へ向けてボボリンクは旅立とうとしている。もう春なのである。季節が移り進め
ば、羽がもっと鮮やかな色あいになるだろう。彼等の歌声が美しく響く。（ジョージア）

春を待つペリカン：Pelicans await the spring

冬ごもりをしていた海辺の地から戻ったばかりのアメリカシロペリカン。彼らは極端なま
でに警戒心が強く、近づき難い存在である。（ワイオミング）

ハスの花咲く頃：Witness to the emergence of lotus blossoms

ハスの花は、日中だけにしか花開くことをしない。太陽がその高みにさしかかった時、シャッターを切ろうとする私の前に、いつのまにかアメリカヘビウがたたずんでいた。（ジョージア）

ねぐら：Evening roost

今にも陽が沈もうとしていた。優に百を越すクロコンドルとヒメコンドルが、冬の夕空を
音もなく飛び回っていた。沼地のはずれにあるねぐらに帰ろうとして……。（フロリダ）

獲物めがけて：Young eagle on Dosewalips marsh

雨にけぶる冬の日。ハクトウワシの子供が急降下してゆく。獲物となるサケが、
川を泳いでいたのだろう。（ワシントン）

エボシクマゲラ：Pileated woodpecker in cypress forest

イトスギの生える沼地。霞がかかり、空はどんよりとしていた。その時、沈んだ周囲の雰囲気を破る
かのように、ひとつがいの大柄なエボシクマゲラが、けたたましい音をたてた。（フロリダ）

モズ：Shrike

曇り空の冬のある日。ふと見ると、沼のほとりに人のような顔をした鳥がいる。アメリカオオモズだ。
しかつめらしいその顔は、距離をおくようにと、私に告げている。（ルイジアナ）

ヤシアメリカムシクイ：Palm warbler in winter reeds

澄みわたった朝。沼のほとり。餌になる昆虫を求めて、ヤシアメリカムシクイがあちらこちらに見えかくれする。
だが、こんなに多くを確認できながらも、私の写真には容易に収まらない不思議さが彼等にはある。（フロリダ）

アカクロムクドリモドキ：Orchard oriole

沼のみぎわに沿ってアカクロムクドリモドキが雌を追いかけながら飛び去ってゆく。枝に羽を休
めるおまえは誰を見送っているのだろうか。（ジョージア）

ここに示されている写真の多くは、アイオワにある私の両親の小さな農場で撮影したものである。農場は人の手の入っていない森の中にあるため、野性の動物たちが、飼い慣らされた動物たちと共存することができる。こうした思いやりのある生活様式が、アメリカの中でどんどん失われつつある。けれども、なお多くの人々が、オウゴンヒワやコウカンチョウの住む小さな農場なり森林なりを保護しようと努力している。

似たような小さな野性区が、北アメリカ全域に点在している。全く地図がなくとも見つけられるほど多い。

イカルが朝に鳴くその声に耳を傾けてみよう。アメリカコガラの群れを追いかけてもみよう。春になれば、西の方からイースタンブルーバード（ルリツグミ）もやってくる。森は鳥たちを喜んで迎え入れてくれるのだ。人々がその存在も知らないような荒野はまだたくさんある。特に、アイオワ、オレゴン、テキサス、オハイオといった州に多い。このような荒野の面影をとどめる場所は、小規模であり、とかく忘れられがちであるけれども、なお残存しており、アメリカが未来にのこす素晴しい遺産になっている。

さらに広範囲にこうした土地を見つけようとするならば、オースチン（ウェストテキサス）の近くにあるヒルカントリーや、グレイトスモーキー山脈（ノースカロライナ）の一部、またはバーモントにある小さな農地などがよいだろう。南の国の面影を求めようとするならば、リオグランデ川（サウステキサス）沿いに開けている地域がよい。メキシコ湾からもほど遠くないところにある。

Many of these photos were taken on my parent's small farm in Iowa within woods they have kept unplowed so that wild animals could share the land with domestic animals. This thoughtful way of life is fast disappearing in America. Yet, many people try to preserve the small farm, the forest, and the wild tangles where goldfinch and cardinals thrive.

Similar, small wild places are scattered throughout North America. You will not need a map of any kind to find them.

Listen for the grosbeak's morning song, follow the chickadee flocks, and watch for the western bluebird's arrival in spring.

The birds know where they are welcome. You will find an abundance of undeclared wilderness within these spaces in Iowa, Oregon, Texas, or Ohio. These remnants of wild land may be small and may seem to be forgotten, but they remain as places of beauty that are among America's greatest treasures.

Larger expanses of these kinds of places can be seen in the Hill Country of West Texas near Austin, within the Great Smokey Mountains of North Carolina, and small farmland of Vermont. The most exotic place lies along the Rio Grande River in South Texas not far from the Gulf of Mexico.

森や農場を抜けて
FOREST AND FARM

森はささやく : Forest whispers at winter's end

スモーキーの山並の中に分け入ってみた。早春のすがすがしさが、ツツジを従えた広葉樹
の森から伝わってきた。（ノースカロライナ）

冬の輝き：Winter brilliance

ショウジョウコウカンチョウは非常に一般的な鳥として、森や農地でよく見られる。厳し
い寒さの中で燃えるように輝いているその姿がまぶしい。（アイオワ）

アメリカカケス：West Texas Jay along the Rio Frio River

早春とはいえ、陽が照りつけると暑い。水浴びでもするつもりなのか、アメリカカケスが
川沿いに飛び交う。あまりに美しい彼等。逃がすまいとする私の気持がゆれる。(テキサス)

ミドリサンジャク：Green jay brightens the Rio Grande morning

リオグランデの朝。一面の雲。森はうつ然としている。その中をぬうようにして、南部の
国境付近でしか見ることのできない、美しいミドリサンジャクが飛ぶ。（テキサス）

野性のクワの実：A taste of wild mulberries

クワの木の上にズアカキツツキを見た。周囲に気を配りながら、用心深くクワの実を食べ
ている。私は音をたてぬように、そっと木のそばに潜んでいた。(アイオワ)

朝の歌：Morning song

淡い春の日。美しい羽色のムネアカイカルが、気持よさそうに歌を
うたっていた。どうやら近くに巣があるようだ。（アイオワ）

草原に憩う：A farmer's retreat

朝早く、名も知らぬ牧草地に来てみた。朝露が消え去る前のひんやりとした静けさ。陽ざしが強まるにつれ、ハッカやアザミの草の息
吹が聞こえてくる。可愛らしいオウゴンヒワ。アザミの種を食べ、生い繁るその中に巣を作る姿がほほえましい。（アイオワ）

テキサスのブルーバード：The bluebird of Texas

明けの空が朱に染まってゆく。樫の枝の上にいるルリツグミが、祈るようにその光景をみ
つめている。（テキサス）

シマセゲラ：Red-bellied woodpecker

冬。厳しい季節である。いつもなら活発であるはずのシマセゲラが、空腹に弱りはてたの
か、今日はいくぶん元気がない。（アイオワ）

ネコマネドリ：Soft meows in briar patch—Catbird

ブライアーの繁みに不思議な鳥がいる。仔ネコのように、にゃあにゃあ鳴く。好奇心の強
いこの鳥は、その名もネコマネドリである。（アイオワ）

コガラ一輪：Chickadee on Whitetail Farm

どんよりとした冬空から、ちらほらと雪が降っていた。素早いものがヤナギの枝をかすめ
たその時、私の目の前には、アメリカコガラの愛らしい花が咲いていた。（アイオワ）

冬の華：Mulberry's winter blossoms

その日、冬の空は見事に晴れわたっていた。だが、つがいのショウジョウコウカンチョウは
折り合いが悪く、この構図で撮るまでにずいぶん待たなければならなかった。（アイオワ）

セジロコゲラ：Downy woodpecker

セジロコゲラはものおじしない小鳥である。ちょっとしたポーズをとるところ
などは、けっこう様になる。（アイオワ）

空高く翼に飛形を与えながら、キジオライチョウが、果てしないワイオミングの冬景色を横切ってゆく。けれども、甘く芳香の漂う春ともなれば、草原の様相は一変する。ソノランデザート同様、この"乾いた土地"の春も、けっして捨てたものではない。

この章のハイライトは、乾燥地に生息する、生命力に溢れた"モーニング・ダンサー"、つまりプレイリーグラウスの仲間たちである。(40ページのキジオライチョウ、P46.47のソウゲンライチョウとホソオライチョウ)この優雅な鳥たちは、毎年の求愛の儀式を全世界に向けられた舞台の上で執り行うかのように演じてくれる。そのダンスを見ると、私たちは昔日の思いに揺さぶられる。西部の草原に獣たちが地響を立てて走っていたあのころに、連れ戻されてしまう。何百万頭ものバイソンやレイヨウ、それにプレイリードッグが、この草原を闊歩していたのだ。今でもなお舞台はその姿をとどめ、草原のダンサーたちは、他にも多くロッキー山脈の東のはずれに生き残っている。

この活気に溢れるダンスを見るための場所としては、ウィロークリークに添ったところが最適だろう。そのウィロークリークが流れ下って高原をぬい、リオグランデ川、スネーク川、プラット川、さらにミズーリ川をかたちづくっているのである。ウインドケイブ国立公園(サウスダコタ)、ポーニー・コマンチ・ナショナル・グラスランズ(コロラド・カンザス)、レッドデザート(ワイオミング)、サハロ・ナショナル・モニュメント(アリゾナ)、ビッグベンド国立公園(テキサス)などを訪れてみるのもよい。

Setting its wings in flight, the sage grouse soars across what seems to be an eternal winter in Wyoming. But, the prairie will offer a sweet, fragrant spring and, like the Sonoran Desert, this dry land is far from deserted.

There is no greater reminder of the exuberance of life within these drylands than the morning dancers—the prairie grouse (Pages 40, 46, and 47). These exquisite birds perform a yearly ritual as if on a stage for all the world. Their dance stirs our memory of the days when western prairies still thundered beneath the feet of many millions of bison, antelope, and prairie dogs. Still, this prairie stage and many other prairie dancers remain along the eastern edge of the Rocky Mountains.

Perhaps the best places to see this dance of life are along the willow creeks that flow down through the higher plateaus to form the Rio Grande, the Snake, the Platte, and the Missouri Rivers. You might visit Wind Cave National Park in South Dakota, Pawnee and Comanche National Grasslands of Colorado and Kansas, the Red Desert of Wyoming, the Saguaro National Monument in Arizona, and Big Bend National Park in Texas.

草原からウィロークリークへ
FROM PRAIRIES TO WILLOW CREEKS

草原からウィロークリークへ
FROM PRAIRIES TO WILLOW CREEKS

モンタナの夕焼け：Montana

まもなく春が終ろうとしている。沈みゆく太陽。大空のキャンバスに描か
れた夕焼けの色あいも、日一日と夏のそれに近づいてゆく。(モンタナ)

赤い草原 : Red grass prairie

秋の初めだというのに、初雪が降った。その雪の下で牧草となるウシクサが、見事なばかりに赤く色づいていた。
ここはかって、バイソン、オオカミ、ハイイログマが我物顔に歩きまわっていた土地だ。（サウスダコタ）

バッタが去った後：When the grasshoppers have gone

冬は近い。雪あらしにも見舞われ、バッタも葉を食べつくしてしまった。アメリカオオモズの心は背景の空のように暗い。（サウスダコタ）

銀嶺に翔く：Winter's vastness

厳寒のある日。キジオライチョウの一群れが、雪におおわれたレッドデザートの上を、力強く翔いていた。（ワイオミング）

もうすぐ春：On Willow Creek—the pink edge of spring

春が色づいてきた。燃えるようなヤナギが美しい。陽ざしの強さを確かめるように、私はゆっくりと歩を運ぶ。（コロラド）　　41

ムナフヒメドリ：Tree sparrow

凍りつくような冬の朝。何げなく目にしたムナフヒメドリにひかれ、私は彼の後を追うことにした。やがて、ヒ
マワリの種を食べているその姿を見い出すと、なぜか私はほっとした。（コロラド）

オウゴンヒワ：Winter goldfinches

29ページの右上の写真のように、雄のオウゴンヒワは夏の間はあざやかな黄色と黒の羽をまとっている。だが、
雪が降り、寒さが厳しくなってくると、その羽の色も背景の冬枯れのように沈んでいく。（コロラド）

春の待人：Waiting for spring

春を待ち望むのは人間ばかりではない。残り少なくなったホリバグミの実を食べるコマツグミや、冬の終わりに卵を生むアメリカワシミミズクもそうである。春になれば……。それは生きとし生けるものの自然な気持かもしれない。（コロラド）

銀色の翼：Silver wings

ヒメレンジャクが群れをなして、枯れ枝の上に羽を休めている。結束の堅い彼等。朝日
を受けるその翼は銀色に輝いて、警固する兵士の鎧をおもわせる。（テキサス）

消えゆく宝：A vanishing treasure

春。北アメリカで最も美しいと言われ、絶滅の危機に瀕しているソウゲンライチョウの雌
が、求愛のダンスをする雄のなわばりに近づいてきた。（カンザス）

一服：A dancer's repose

これみよがしに片足でダンスをするホソオライチョウたち。でも、雨
の朝は気分が今一つのらないようだ。まずは一休み。（ネブラスカ）

羽色淡く：Say's phoebe

陽が昇る時、鳥たちがその荘厳な一瞬に見つめ入るのはなぜなのだろう。草やぐらの上から、今日もセイズフェーベ（チャイロツキヒメハエトリ）は見ていた。（テキサス）

これより西部：Where the west begins

サボテンの枝に、マルハシツグミモドキが止まっている。西部の香りが漂う。（アリゾナ）

マガモ一羽：One mallard

アメリカでは、マガモが全域に住んでいる。平凡ではあるが、処世術を身につけた生命力の強い鳥ともいえる。（コロラド）

ヤナギの花：Willow blossoms

ヤナギの花の柔らかな美しさに誘われて、小鳥たちがやってくる。写真はニシフウキンチョウとキヅタアメリカムシクイ。春の朝の優しいひととき。（ジョージア）

昇ったばかりの朝の太陽から放たれた、暖かな光の条が、じんわりとガマの穂を照らし、羽根を休めているサギの姿を温め始めると、柔かなトンボの羽音が、夏の朝の沈黙を破る。ほどなく、ザブンという音がして、カイツブリやアヒルが水の中に飛び込むのがわかる。キガラシムクドリモドキが歌い、鳥の羽毛が朝日に染まって金色に輝く。

立ち止まってみよう。黄金色に映えるムクドリモドキが、ガマの繁みの中にある止り木の上で、歌をうたっているのが聞こえてくる。また、高山の中にある沼地のまわりを歩いてみよう。たとえば、イエローストーン公園や、コロラドロッキーでもいい。それとも、高山から流れ下ってくる、川のあたりを歩いてみることにしようか。そうすれば、このような場所の不思議なおもしろさに、自分たちの心が、何度となく引きつけられてゆくのがわかるはずだ。それはガン、マガモ、さらにはあの優雅なハクチョウまでが、まるでムクドリモドキの歌声に誘われたかのように、山の中の水辺に集まってくる光景に本当によく似ている。

気軽に訪ねられる西部の沼地としては、ワイオミング州ジャクソンのはずれにある、国立エルク保護区があげられる。同様にコロラド州ノースパークのウォールデンの近く、あるいはオレゴン州のマルーア国立野生動物保護区にある、いくつかの沼地がおもしろいだろう。

As the glow from the first, warm rays of morning sun filters through the cattails to warm the silent heron, a soft whir of dragonfly wings breaks the summer silence. Soon, you hear the splash of grebes and ducks. Then, a yellow-headed blackbird sings and the sun comes to life in the bird's golden feathers.

Stop when you hear this golden bird sing from its perch in the cattails. Walk the edges of the high mountain marshes of Yellowstone Park, the Colorado Rockies, or the edge of a river winding down from the higher peaks. You will be drawn again and again to the magic of these places just as the blackbird's song seems to invite the geese, the mallards, and the elegant swans that stop within the mountain marsh each year.

You can easily visit these western marshes within the National Elk Refuge on the edge of Jackson, Wyoming. Also, visit marshes near the town of Walden in North Park, Colorado or those within Malheur National Wildlife Refuge in Oregon.

沼地にて
MARSH

沼地にて
MARSH

白鳥の湖：Swan Lake

木々の間からレッドロック湖が見える。ナキハクチョウの多くが巣
作りをする水のふるさとである。(モンタナ)

カナダヅル：Sandhill crane

カナダヅルの独特な鳴き声が響く。その度に春の陽ざしは強まり、沼地の朝は活気に満ちてくる。（モンタナ）

夏トンボ：Dragonfly in soft summer light

夏、照りつける陽の光。トンボが羽音も高く飛び去る。そして、再び同じ場所へ戻ってくる。羽虫をつかまえようとしているのだ。（コロラド）

水鏡：An avocet's elegant reflection

アメリカソリハシセイタカシギが、凍った池に映る自分の姿に見入っている。朝化粧を終え、そのできばえを確かめでもするように。（コロラド）

黒歌鳥：Marsh gold

ガマの繁みの中に、キガラシムクドリモドキがいる。西部の湖沼に住み、その地では中心となる鳥である。（コロラド）

翼を休めて：Migrant's perch

曇りがちな春の朝。はるか北へ向けて旅立つキガラシムクドリモドキが、枝の上に舞い降り、しばしの休息をとっている。（モンタナ）

草笛のシンフォニー：Marsh symphony

夏になった。しかし、どんなに強烈に太陽が照りつけようとも、ハゴロモガラスの快活な歌声はやまない。（ジョージア）

オオホシハジロとオナガガモ：Canvasbacks and Northern pintails

春になるとオオホシハジロやオナガガモなど渡り鳥たちの北帰行が始まる。住み慣れた水辺を去る前のくつろいだ時間だ。（オレゴン）

休息：A weary migrant family

春の野辺に下り立つマガン。飢えと疲れをいやす彼らの姿は、もの静かで何ともいえない美しさがある。（オレゴン）

ナキハクチョウ：Trumpeter swan

雪が溶け、すっかり春めいてきた。やわらかな春の光の中に浮かび上がるナキハクチョウの姿は見るものを魅きつけてやまない。（ワイオミング）

アメリカヒドリ：Winter wigeons

寒さの厳しい冬のある日。背を丸めてアメリカヒドリが眠っている。ぴったりと身を寄せ合い、安心しきった様子で。（コロラド）

春の羽音：The sound of spring……

夕日の沈むその時を合図に、ハクガンがいっせいに飛び立った。空に舞う力強い羽音。壮大な明暗。私は胸の高鳴りを押えることができなかった。（オレゴン）

ハクガン：and rush of wings—snow geese

ハクガンは翼をかたむけて、北へ進路をとった。彼等の前方にはカナダがひらけ、ロシアが横たわっている。（オレゴン）

優雅に漂う：The soft beauty……

ナキハクチョウがうなだれている。灰白色のキャンバスに、冬の詩情が溢れる。（ワイオミング）

ハクチョウ：of swans

厳しくつらい季節を生き抜くために、ナキハクチョウはここ、スワンズ・レイクで冬を越す。かつては
あれほど隆盛を誇っていた彼等も、今では数千羽を確認できるだけになってしまった。（ワイオミング）

東方へ：Flight to the East

春霞の中を連れ添う2羽のカナダガン。振り下ろす翼のリズムも整
然と、彼等は見事な調和を見せていた。（コロラド）

ひとつがい：A moment of eternity

カナダガンを撮り始めて３年。恥じらうようにうつむき、それでいてぴったりと寄りそう
彼等の姿の美しさに、私は近づいているのだろうか。（コロラド）

影の絵巻：Majestic symbols of……

陽の光の最初の一条が、雲のすきまから差し込むと、燃え立つ炎に照らし出されるように、
水辺には明と暗が起伏する。（コロラド）

新世界：a new wilderness

言葉では描けなかった詩情がある。カメラでは捉えられなかった美しさがある。カナダガンを目の前
にすると、いつの間にか私は、感動を通り越して息苦しさを覚えてしまう。（コロラド）

仲間たち：Harmony

冬の朝、水煙の立ち込めるその中を、お互いに声をかけ、一羽また一羽と仲間のいる場所に集まってくる。（コロラド）

再会：Returning to the flock

嬉しさを全身で表現しながら、群れの中に舞い下りてゆく数羽。彼等の鳴き交わす声には、胸にせまるものがある。（コロラド）

旅立ち：Flight

春の気配があたりに漂い始めるころ曇り空の中を、再び北へ向けて彼等は飛び立ってゆく。（コロラド）

安らぎ：Serenity

春のうららかなある日。長い長い首をもたげて、一羽のオオアオサギが、野原でのんびり日向ぼっこをしていた。（ジョージア）

雪が降り始める頃や、冬のなごりが消え去ろうとする頃に、マウンテンブルーバードは姿を現わす。空から舞い下りてくるその様子は、一切れの夏空のように鮮かだ。

ロッキーの山並みの中、私たちの生活空間から遠くはなれたところで、マウンテンブルーバードは生まれる。ここにはその他、アオライチョウやヒメレンジャク、ギンザンマシコといった鳥たちが、それぞれの王国を構えて住んでいる。しかし、ブルーバードはこれら他の鳥たちとは異なり、1ケ所に滞まって冬を迎えるようなことはしない。彼らは南へと旅立ってゆく。おそらく、ニューメキシコ、アリゾナ、メキシコといった方面にであろう。にもかかわらず、一度な

らずブルーバードを見かけたり、また、その容姿に心を動かされたりした人々にとって、ブルーバードの神々しいまでの美しさは、いつまでも胸の内から消えることはない。その美しさを通して、人々は山それ自体にも強烈な思いを抱くようになるのである。

ノーザンアルバータからメキシコまでマウンテンブルーバードを追い続けながら、ロッキー山脈をぐるりと巡ってみよう。ブルーバードの巣作りが見られる場所としては、イエローストーン国立公園とロッキーマウンテン国立公園が最適だろう。

冬になって私たちは、ブルーバードを探し求めた。けれども、彼らの正確な居所は、今もって謎なのである……。

During the first snowfall or during winter's last traces, the mountain bluebird might appear, dropping from above like a piece of summer sky.

Here in the Rocky Mountains, so far from our daily lives, mountain bluebirds are born. Here too, the blue grouse, waxwings, and pine grosbeaks dwell in this mountain kingdom. Yet, the bluebird, unlike these other birds, will not remain when winter returns. They will journey to the south, maybe into New Mexico, Arizona, or Mexico. Still, for those who

have seen them at any time of year and have been touched by their presence, the majestic beauty of bluebirds will remain in the heart, bringing the mountain home.

Follow the mountain bluebirds along the entire Rocky Mountain chain from Northern Alberta to Mexico. The best places to see nesting bluebirds are within Yellowstone National Park and Rocky Mountain National Park. We have searched for them in winter and their exact whereabouts remains a mystery to us.....

山、マウンテンブルーバードの故郷へ
MOUNTAIN

山、マウンテンブルーバードの故郷へ
MOUNTAIN

初雪 : Soft brush of winter

初雪が降った。まもなく本格的な冬が来る。秋の残り香を淡く漂わ
せながら、木々はすでに冬の気配を感じている。（ワイオミング）

アスペンの緑：Aspen's soft glow

　　　　木々の輝きに心魅かれて分け入ってみようとする時、森の誘惑はもう始まっている。（モンタナ）

ニシフウキンチョウ：Golden tanager

長い時間、辛抱に辛抱を重ねて私は待っていた。だが、ニシフウキンチョウは、アスペン
の枝に舞い下りたかと思うまもなく、視界から消え去っていた。（モンタナ）

森の中：In the forest's depths

アスペンの木立の中は、静寂に包まれていた。春霞の淡いベールのかかるその奥には、お
とぎ話の世界への秘密の扉が隠されている。（モンタナ）

瑠璃色の眺め：Lazuli's gaze

ホオジロの仲間であるムネアカルリノジコを見つけた。滅多に出会うことのない被写体で
あり、撮り終えて私は無性に嬉しかったことを覚えている。（モンタナ）

ビャクシンの上で：On the old juniper

雨の中で写真を撮るのは至難の技である。カメラを台無しにしてまでも撮ろうとしたニシ
フウキンチョウ。私にとっては、それほどまでに価値があった。（モンタナ）

ギンザンマシコ：Pine grosbeak's mountain kingdom

夏。つい先ほどまで降っていた雨が止んだ。仲間からはぐれたギンザンマシコが、ブンゲ
ンス・トウヒの木の上で、森の気配を探っている。（コロラド）

ヒメハジロのいる小川：Bufflehead Creek

肌寒い曇りかげんの秋の午後。小川の土手のコヨーテが、物欲しそうな顔をして、ヒメハジロの動きを見守っていた。（ワイオミング）

ヒメレンジャク：Cedar waxwing

太陽が今にも沈もうとしていた。そして、ヒメレンジャクたちは今にも消え去ろうとしていた。
私は、転げるようにして山腹を駆け下り、夢中でシャッターを押し続けた。（テキサス）

タカの子供：Young hawk

雪が降っていた日。オウゴンヒワを食べ終えたばかりのアシボソハイタカを見た。若鳥といえども、
その圧倒するような威風には、冬の寒さを喰いちぎるような迫力があった。（コロラド）

キビタイシメとアオライチョウ：Evening grosbeak and Blue grouse

陽の光がさんさんと降り注いでいる。鳥たちにとって春は大きな意味を持つ。タソガレシ
メの目に、アオライチョウの目に、日一日と力強さが増してゆく。（ワイオミング）

マウンテンブルーバード：Mountain bluebirds

初めてマウンテンブルーバード（ムジルリツグミ）の美しさをカメラにおさめようとしたのが1982年。
あれから長い時間が経って、ようやく私はここ、ロッキー山脈で彼との再会を果たした。（コロラド）

ユッカの花 : The first yucca blossom of spring

ユッカの種さやを破って、マウンテンブルーバードが生まれ出た。春の空の中へ、生まれて
初めての飛行を試みようとしているもののように、風の向きをうかがっている。(コロラド)

途方にくれて：Migrant's discontent

ファインダーを覗いた瞬間、ブルーバードの途方に暮れたような顔が飛び込んできた。故郷へ帰ってきたというのに、何が不満なのだろうか。（コロラド）

ビロードモウズイカの繁みにて：Bluebird in mullein forest

幸せの青い鳥が、目の前で美しい瑠璃色の花に生まれ変わった。約2年の間、この花を咲かせ
ようとしては果たせず、空しく歩きまわったが、ようやく報われた思いである。（コロラド）

冬枯れ：Soft patterns at winter's end

春とはいえ、冬の寒さがまだ残る。冬枯れの背景に、ぽつんと、夏の青い空の切れ端をはりつけたような一枚である。（コロラド）

撮影メモ Photographic Notes

COASTAL SWAMP

9 Kingfisher in a Northwest salt marsh, Washington
Kingfishers are common throughout America and are always a joy to see, whether in a Florida orange grove or in the depths of a mangrove swamp. This photograph was taken on an overcast day as this Kingfisher was searching for small fish.
Nikon FM2 Nikkor 400mm F3.5 f4 1/125

10 Great and Snowy egrets, Georgia
This photograph was taken on an early spring day near the Savannah River. It was early in the morning and the birds were feeding as the tide went out.
I had never seen so many egrets, herons, storks and ibises feeding in one place. These are normally solitary birds, gathering at most in small groups. I watched these birds for as long as possible trying to better understand them as a group.
Nikon FM2 Nikkor 400mm F3.5 f4 1/500

11 Roseate Spoonbills, Louisiana
Here again I was photographing wildlife on an early, rainy spring day. The soft, pink feathers of the Roseate Spoonbills are extremely beautiful, but to appreciate them fully the day should be misty and gray. The difficult part in taking this picture was that it was so cold and I stood in one place for so long that I could barely depress the shutter button.
Nikon FM2 Nikkor 400mm F3.5 f3.5 1/60

12 Least Bittern, Georgia
Least Bitterns are a joy to watch, if you can discover them in their habitat. But Bitterns are extremely secretive, and when they are disturbed will blend in as much as possible with the surrounding marsh grasses. They can appear very much like the vegetation. The only place I have seen very many of these is on the Savannah National Wildlife Refuge in Georgia.
Nikon FM2 Nikkor 400mm F3.5 f5.6 1/250

13 Bobolink, Georgia
Bobolinks nest on small farms and in large grasslands, but they are commonly seen in coastal marshes during migration. This photograph was taken on a spring day when the Bobolinks were heading further north.
This bird has a beautiful song. As the season progresses the Bobolink will grow more colorful.
Nikon FM2 Nikkor 400mm F3.5 f8 1/250

14 American White Pelicans, Wyoming
White birds, such as pelicans, are best photographed on cloudy days. These birds had probably just arrived from their coastal wintering grounds. American White Pelicans are extremly wary and thus difficult to approach.
Nikon FM2 Nikkor 400mm F3.5 f4 1/125

15 Anhinga, Georgia
Lotus blossoms only open during the middle of the day, so this photograph had to be taken when the sun was at its highest point. Anhinga's dive for fish, much like cormorants, but are only found in the southeastern United States.
Nikon FM2 Nikkor 400mm F3.5 f8 1/250

16 Black and Turkey Vultures, Florida
The sun was just setting when I took this picture. There were hundreds of vultures gliding in the winter sky, coming down to roost at the edge of a swamp.
Nikon FM2 Nikkor 400mm F3.5 f5.6 1/250

17 Young American Bald Eagle, Washington
This young bald eagle is swooping down on chum salmon swimming in the salt marsh. The photograph was taken on a rainy, winter's day.
Nikon FM2 Nikkor 400mm F3.5 f4 1/250

18 Pileated Woodpecker in cypress swamp, Florida
A pair of these large woodpeckers was making a great deal of noise on this hazy, overcast day.
Nikon FM2 Nikkor 400mm F3.5 f3.5 1/60

19 Loggerhead Shrike, Louisiana
Shrikes spend their summers farther to the north, where they are common on our prairies. They are also extremely difficult to approach. This photograph was taken on a cloudy winter's day at the edge of a swamp.
Nikon FM2 Nikkor 400mm F3.5 f3.5 1/125

20 Palm Warbler, Florida
Palm Warblers spend the winter in Florida, but nest in Canada. This photograph was taken in a swamp, on a sunny morning in January. The Warblers were everywhere, searching for insects. It was difficult to find one that would stop for a second while I took his photograph.
Nikon FM2 Nikkor 400mm F3.5 f5.6 1/250

21 Orchard Oriole, Georgia
Male Orchard Orioles were chasing females and getting into fights with each other on this early spring day. A great many of these birds were migrating along the edge of a swamp.
Nikon FM2 Nikkor 400mm F3.5 f5.6 1/125

FOREST AND FARM

23 Hardwood forest with an understory of rhododendrons, North Carolina
An early spring day in the Smokey Mountains. The largest unbroken tracts of hardwood forest in America are found in the Smokies.
Nikon FM2 Nikkor 80-200mm F4 f8 1/125

24 Northern Cardinal, Iowa
Cardinals are best photographed on cloudy days when you can better see the brilliant red of their feathers. These are extremely common birds in our eastern forests and farmlands. This photograph was taken on a very cold winter's day.
Nikon FM2 Nikkor 400mm F3.5 f4 1/125

25 Scrub Jay, Texas
All jays are extremely curious. Scrub Jays are exceptionally beautiful birds, but it is hard to do them justice in a photograph. It was a hot, sunny spring morning when I took this picture.
Nikon FM2 Nikkor 400mm F3.5 f8 1/125

26 Green Jay, Texas
This photograph was taken on an overcast day in a forest along the Rio Grande River. Green Jays are only found along the very southern boundary of the United States, here at the border between Mexico and Texas. These are beautiful birds.
Nikon FM2 Nikkor 400mm F3.5 f3.5 1/125

27 Red-headed Woodpecker in mulberry tree, Iowa
This photograph was taken on an extremely dark, over-cast day. Red-headed Woodpeckers are very wary, so I stood quietly by this wild mulberry tree until one came to eat the berries.
Nikon FM2 Nikkor 400mm F3.5 f3.5 1/125

28 Rose-breasted Grosbeak, Iowa
Rose-breasted Grosbeaks are as beautiful as the small farms and woods where they live. They have fine feathers and a lovely song.
This photograph was taken on a hazy spring day. The bird's mate had a nest nearby.
Nikon FM2 Nikkor 400mm F3.5 f5.6 1/500

29 Top left/American Goldfinch on thistle, Iowa
Top right/American Goldfinch, Iowa
Bottom left/Grasses, Iowa
Bottom right/Mint, Iowa
All four of these photographs were taken in the back pasture of my parent's farm, where mint grows in abundance. There is nothing like the beauty of a pasture early in the morning when the dew is on the grass.
Goldfinches are Iowa's state bird and a symbol of the small farm. They eat thistle seeds and nest in thistle plants.
Top left/Nikon FM2 Nikkor 400mm F3.5 f5.6 1/125
Top right, bottom left, bottom right/Nikon FM2 Nikkor 400mm F3.5 f5.6 1/250

30 Male Eastern Bluebird in oak tree, Texas
Very early in the morning, just as the sun was rising, I discovered these Eastern Bluebirds wintering in the hill country of east Texas. Bluebirds and

Bald Eagles are probably more difficult to photograph than any other birds.
Nikon FM2 Nikkor 400mm F3.5 f4 1/125

31 Red-bellied Woodpecker, Iowa
Woodpeckers, and especially Red-bellied Woodpeckers, seem to have softer feathers than all other birds. Red-bellied Woodpeckers are extremely wary.
Nikon FM2 Nikkor 400mm F3.5 f8 1/250

32 Gray Catbird, Georgia
Catbirds are one of the most common birds on an Iowa farm, and probably the most common in American briar patches. Their soft meows sound like kittens. They are extremely curious.
Left/Nikon FM2 Nikkor 400mm F3.5 f4 1/125
Right/Nikon FM2 Nikkor 400mm F3.5 f4 1/250

33 Black-capped Chickadee, Iowa
This photograph was taken on a cloudy winter day when the snow was falling. On an Iowa farm the most pleasing sound on a winter day is chicka-dee-dee. Here, the chickadee was sitting on a willow branch. Chickadees move so rapidly they are extremely difficult to photograph on a cloudy day.
Nikon FM2 Nikkor 400mm F3.5 f4 1/125

34 Northern Cardinal pair in mulberry tree, Iowa
Cardinals add color to an Iowa farm in winter. But getting a pair to sit for a photograph takes time and patience.
Nikon FM2 Nikkor 400mm F3.5 f8 1/250

35 Downy Woodpecker, Iowa
Downy Woodpeckers are found throughout the United States. They are friendly little birds.
Nikon FM2 Nikkor 400mm F3.5 f4 1/60

FROM PRAIRIES TO WILLOW CREEKS

37 Sunset, Montana
This sunset appeared after a spring rain shower. It is typical of the western American sunset, where the sky does not seem to be big enough to contain all the beauty.
Nikon FM2 Nikkor 80-200mm F4 f4 1/125

38 Red grass prairie, South Dakota
This photograph was taken after the first snow of the year in early fall. The red grass in the photograph is big bluestem.
This is the type of prairie that was home to bison, wolves, grizzly bears and sharp-tailed grouse.
Nikon FM2 Nikkor 80-200mm F4 f5.6 1/125

39 Loggerhead Shrike, South Dakota

Shrikes eat grasshoppers and mice during the summer. When the grasshoppers and mice have gone they migrate to the south.
Nikon FM2 Nikkor 400mm F3.5 f5.6 1/125

40 Sage Grouse, Wyoming
The Red Desert is in western Wyoming. It is a very inhospitable place in winter, and the day I took this picture it was extremely cold.
Nikon FM2 Nikkor 400mm F3.5 f5.6 1/500

41 Willow Creek, Colorado
Willows begin to change color in late winter, becoming more and more beautiful until the Willow blossoms appear.
Nikon FM2 Nikkor 80-200mm F4 f11 1/125

42 Left/Tree Sparrow in rabbitbrush, Colorado
Right/Tree Sparrow on sunflower, Colorado
Tree Sparrows are probably the most beautiful of all American sparrows, or at least they are my favorites.
Left/Nikon FM2 Nikkor 400mm F3.5 f4 1/60
Right/Nikon FM2 Nikkor 400mm F3.5 f5.6 1/250

43 Left/American Goldfinch on sunflower, Colorado
Right/American Goldfinches on sunflower, Colorado
Male American Goldfinches are bright yellow and black in the summer, but become like the landscape in winter. This picture was taken just after a snowfall, and is one of my favorites.
One of the Goldfinches from the right picture returned for this picture. There is often one bird which is tamer than others.
Nikon FM2 Nikkor 400mm F3.5 f4 1/250

44 Left/American Robins in Russian olive tree, Colorado
Right/Great Horned Owl in cottonwood tree, Colorado
It seems strange to think of owls and robins together, since owls are creatures of the night and robins remind us of the sunniest summer days. But these photographs were taken on a cold winter's day, when both birds seemed to be waiting for spring.
Left/Nikon FM2 Nikkor 400mm F3.5 f5.6 1/250
Right/Nikon FM2 Nikkor 400mm F3.5 f11 1/125

45 Cedar Waxwings, Texas
This photograph was taken just at sunrise. Waxwings rarely leave the security of their flock. The spectacular beauty of these birds can be appreciated in a photograph like this one.
Nikon FM2 Nikkor 400mm F3.5 f3.5 1/60

46 Lesser Pinnated Grouse, Kansas
This photograph was taken before sunrise as the female Lesser Pinnated Grouse arrived on the males' dancing grounds.

There is no greater pleasure for me than to sleep in a blind on the Lesser Pinnated Grouse lek and to awaken before dawn to the eerie sound of their song. It is like the spirits of a great many Indians have returned from the dead. These birds are among the most beautiful in North America, and in serious danger of being exterminated.
Nikon FM2 Nikkor 400mm F3.5 f3.5 1/125

47 Sharp-tailed Grouse, Nebraska
Sharp-tailed Grouse look like computer wind-up dolls when they dance their mating dance.
Nikon FM2 Nikkor 400mm F3.5 f4 1/60

48 Say's Phoebe, Texas
This photograph was taken just as the sun rose. Say's Phoebes, at least in winter, are very quiet birds, whose soft feathers seem to be part of their personalities.
Nikon FM2 Nikkor 400mm F3.5 f5.6 1/125

49 Curve-billed Thrashers in cholla cactus, Arizona
All thrashers have personalities that are hard to resist. They seem to be very intelligent human beings, rather than birds. This photo was taken on a sunny winter's day as the birds sat in the shade of a cactus.
Nikon FM2 Nikkor 400mm F3.5 f8 1/250

50 Mallard drake, Colorado
Mallards are the most common duck in America, seen quite frequently, but the beauty of these birds is always surprising.
Nikon FM2 Nikkor 400mm F3.5 f11 1/125

51 Top/Western Tanager in willow, Montana
I waited for hours for a Western Tanager to land at this spot. I only had time to click the shutter before he flew on.
Nikon FM2 Nikkor 400mm F3.5 f5.6 1/250

Bottom /Myrtle Warbler, Georgia
This photograph was taken just at sunrise on a spring morning when the willows had just begun to flower.
Myrtle Warblers are probably the tamest of all American Warblers, but still they move so quickly they are difficult to photograph.
Nikon FM2 Nikkor 400mm F3.5 f4 1/250

MARSH

53 Red Rocks Lake, Montana
Red Rocks Lake is the home of a large population of Trumpeter Swans. It is always alive with the sounds of the marsh, and a spectacular place in the spring and summer. This photograph was taken on a misty morning.
Nikon FM2 Nikkor 80-200mm F4 f8 1/125

54 Sandhill Crane, Montana
Sandhill Cranes liven up marsh mornings with their distinctive call. Although these birds fit into any landscape they occupy, getting close enough to photograph them is difficult, because they are still hunted.
Ninkon FM2 Nikkor 400mm F3.5 f5.6 1/250

55 Dragonfly in cattails, Colorado
This dragonfly acted as if he wanted his photograph taken. He kept returning to the same spot to catch insects, and luckily I caught him in flight. Try as I might, I have never again been able to photograph a dragonfly in flight.
Nikon FM2 Nikkor 400mm F3.5 f3.5 1/1000

56 American Avocet, Colorado
On this particular day the avocets had very few places to feed, since the marsh they had come to feed upon was still frozen. So I waited by a small patch of open water, taking the opportunity to get close to these difficult to photograph birds.
Nikon FM2 Nikkor 400mm F3.5 f3.5 1/125

57 Yellow-headed Blackbird in cattails, Colorado
Yellow-headed Blackbirds are the heart and soul of the western marsh. They most often nest in colonies in cattails and reeds along a pond or lake. They are often very tame birds, and on this sunny summer day they were a pleasure to photograph.
Nikon FM2 Nikkor 400mm F3.5 f8 1/250

58 Yellow-headed Blackbirds, Montana
During migration Yellow-headed Blackbirds are often seen in places where they do not seem to belong. But their yellow heads add brilliance to any migration stopover.
Nikon FM2 Nikkor 400mm F3.5 f4 1/60

59 Red-winged Blackbird, Georgia
Red-winged Blackbirds are found in marshes and fields throughout America. If there is one song that is America's song, it is the song of the red-winged blackbird.
Nikon FM2 Nikkor 400mm F3.5 f5.6 1/250

60 Canvasbacks and Northern Pintails, Oregon
Canvasbacks used to be extremely abundant in America, but they are still being hunted and now not often seen. These ducks have just begun their northward journey.
Nikon FM2 Nikkor 400mm F3.5 f4 1/60

61 White-fronted Geese, Oregon
This photograph was taken on a cloudy spring day. White-fronted Geese are very shy and difficult to approach. It is hard to do justice to these beautiful birds with just a photograph.
Nikon FM2 Nikkor 400mm F3.5 f4 1/125

62 Trumpeter Swan, Wyoming
The Trumpeter Swan is an elegant bird that never fails to impress the beholder.
Nikon FM2 Nikkor 400mm F3.5 f4 1/60

63 American Wigeon, Colorado
It is very rewarding to see that an animal is comfortable enough, in my presence, to fall asleep.
Nikon FM2 Nikkor 400mm F3.5 f11 1/125

64 · 65 Snow Geese, Oregon
When in the middle of one of these large flocks of snow geese it is nearly impossible to hear anything other than the sound of their wings and their calls. It is like being in a very loud snowstorm.
This photograph was taken close to sunset on a spring day. These birds were stopping over on their northward migration to Russia and Canada.
Nikon FM2 Nikkor 400mm F3.5 f3.5 1/125

66 · 67 Trumpeter Swans, Wyoming
This photograph was taken on an extremely cold winter's day. These swans were wintering on this warm water stream.
Trumpeter Swans were once extremely abundant in America, but now there are only a few thousand of these birds left. The best place to see them is in Yellowstone National Park.
Nikon FM2 Nikkor 400mm F3.5 f3.5 1/60

68 Canada Geese, Colorado
This photograph was taken on a misty spring morning. Canada Geese mate for life.
Nikon FM2 Nikkor 400mm F3.5 f4 1/250

69 Canada Geese, Colorado
I spent three years photographing Canada Geese, and found their beauty to be the most difficult among all birds to capture.
Nikon FM2 Nikkor 400mm F3.5 f5.6 1/250

70 Canada Geese, Colorado
This photograph was taken on a very cold winter's day. The first rays of sunlight were beginning to reach this warm water pond.
Nikon FM2 Nikkor 400mm F3.5 f4 1/250

71 Canada Geese, Colorado
This photograph was taken in the same spot as the photograph on page 70, but one year later.
Nikon FM2 Nikkor 400mm F3.5 f8 1/500

72 · 73 Canada Geese, Colorado
The heart quickens, and mind delights, but words cannot express the beauty of
Canada Geese.
72 Nikon FM2 Nikkor 80-200mm F4 f5.6 1/500
73 Nikon FM2 Nikkor 80-200mm F4 f8 1/500

74 Canada Geese, Colorado
In America the sight of a flying flock of Canada Geese means that either
spring is in the air or winter is about to begin. Their honking call is one of the
most uplifting of all bird calls.
Nikon FM2 Nikkor 400mm F3.5 f4 1/500

75 Great Blue Heron, Georgia
To me the Great Blue Heron is the essence of patience and serenity, the
grandfather of the marsh. These wonderful birds are found throughout the
United States.
Nikon FM2 Nikkor 400mm F3.5 f5.6 1/250

MOUNTAIN

77 Early Autumn, Wyoming
This photograph was taken on a fall day, after the first snowfall of the year.
The aspens around Swan Lake in Yellowstone have not yet shed their golden
leaves.
Nikon FM2 Nikkor 400mm F3.5 f5.6 1/60

78 Aspens, Montana
Aspens are the most peaceful of all trees. There is a magic about them, a kind
of fairy-tale feeling. This photograph was taken on a hazy spring morning.
Nikon FM2 Nikkor 400mm F3.5 f5.6 1/125

79 Western Tanager in aspen, Montana
Western Tanagers were everywhere on this particular morning. However,
waiting for one to come down from the tops of the aspens took a lot of
patience. This tanager flew a split second after his photograph was taken.
Nikon FM2 Nikkor 400mm F3.5 f4 1/250

80 Aspens, Montana
An inviting aspen forest.
Nikon FM2 Nikkor 400mm F3.5 f4 1/125

81 Lazuli Bunting, Montana
I rarely ever see Lazuli Buntings, so I was extremely pleased to take this
picture. They are beautiful birds.
Nikon FM2 Nikkor 400mm F3.5 f5.6 1/250

82 Western Tanager in juniper, Montana
It is very difficult to photograph animals in rain without destroying your

camera equipment. This photograph was taken on a rainy spring morning.
The junipers have a character all their own.
Nikon FM2 Nikkor 400mm F3.5 f4 1/60

83 Pine Grosbeak in blue spruce, Colorado
This bird is trying to get in touch with the other members of its flock.
Nikon FM2 Nikkor 400mm F3.5 f4 1/125

84 Pelican Creek, Wyoming
This photograph was taken on a cold, cloudy, fall afternoon. The coyote in
this photograph is looking at a female Bufflehead.
Nikon FM2 Nikkor 80-200mm F4 f4 1/125

85 Cedar Waxwings, Texas
I saw this photograph from a great distance away and had to hurry down a
mountain to get it before the sun set. A really beautiful group of birds.
Nikon FM2 Nikkor 400mm F3.5 f5.6 1/250

86 Sharp-shinned Hawk, Colorado
Hawks of all kinds are very difficult to approach, because they are not at all
comfortable around people. Since this was a young bird he was a little easier
to approach. It was snowing here, and the hawk had just eaten a goldfinch.
Nikon FM2 Nikkor 400mm F3.5 f3.5 1/60

87 Top/Evening Grosbeak in juniper, Colorado
Bottom/Blue Grouse, Wyoming
Evening Grosbeaks stay together in flocks, and if one bird gets excited they all
fly away. The Grosbeaks in top photograph are eating juniper berries.
Blue Grouse are abundant in the spring above Slough Creek in Yellowstone
National Park. This grouse had finished displaying to a female grouse.
Top/Nikon FM2 Nikkor 400mm F3.5 f5.6 1/250
Bottom/Nikon FM2 Nikkor 400mm F3.5 f5.6 1/250

88 Mountain Bluebirds and yucca, Colorado
89 Male Mountain Bluebird on yucca seed pod, Colorado
All of these photographs from here on were taken on a cloudy spring day.
Before taking these photographs, I had spent nearly two years unsuccessfully
attempting to photograph mountain bluebirds. It takes a long time to do justice
to such a beautiful bird.
88 Nikon FM2 Nikkor 400mm F3.5 f4 1/60
89 Nikon FM2 Nikkor 400mm F3.5 f4 1/125

90 Mountain Bluebirds on yucca, Colorado
91 Mountain Bluebirds on mullein, Colorado
Mountain Bluebirds breed from Alaska to the mountains of Arizona and New
Mexico. They nest in holes in trees or in nest boxes. They have from four to
six young and the young are fed and raised by both parents. The adults are
exceptionally good parents, as I have seen them chase hawks and ground

squirrels away from their nests.
91 Nikon FM2 Nikkor 400mm F3.5 f4 1/125
92 Nikon FM2 Nikkor 400mm F3.5 f5.6 1/125

92 Female Mountain Bluebird, Colorado
In the fall and spring they often form flocks of from 50 to 200 bluebirds. They winter from southern Colorado and Oregon south. In northern Colorado they are among the first migrants in late March, so they often get caught in snowstorms.
Nikon FM2 Nikkor 400mm F3.5 f4 1/125

FILM——Kodachrome 64

マウンテンブルーバードと私

ずいぶん長い間、野生動物を観察し、その生態の研究を続けてきた。自身の手で動物たちの世話をしたこともある。そうした彼等の姿を写真に撮り始めたのは、かなり後になってからだった。生物学者である私は、私の撮る動物たちがどのように行動するか、どんな生活を送っていて、どんなふうに子供を育てるのかを熟知している。そのため私の写真は、それぞれの動物たちの生態の、相違点も共通点もとらえているように思う。彼等に対する深い思いも、そこにはこめられている。

マウンテンブルーバードの類いまれな美しさに出会ったとき、私は悟った。私の動物たちに対する思いを他の人と分かちあう方法をようやく見つけたのだと。あの輝くような羽根の色、小さな体が伝える魅力。誰の目にもその美しさは明らかである。彼等を見ていると、微笑さえ浮かんでくる。私の体験したあの感情が、見る人すべての心の奥底によみがえってくる。

実際、マウンテンブルーバードは独特の気高さを持っている。そしてこの気高さ、雄々しさを見てとった者には、素晴しいことが待っている。そう、まさにその時からあなたは、他の動物を見ても今までとはちがったとらえ方をしている自分に気づくはずなのである。私の写真から、読者諸氏が、他の鳥たちのそれぞれの美しさをも見てとっていただければ、と願っている。森や農場、あるいは山間部に住み、思い思いの生活を営んでいる鳥たちの美しさを。

この本を私の妻、ジーンと両親、そして文章を書いてくれたロン・ハーシュに捧げたい。カール・シーヴァー、マーク・ルークス、リンダ・ヘルム、ベティ・リンスキー、マルガリーテ・クローニンにも感謝の意を表したいと思う。

THE MOUNTAIN BLUEBIRDS AND I

After many years of watching, caring for, and studying animals, I began to photograph them. As a biologist, I knew there were photos I could take that would show people differences between animals, their behavior, and where they live and raise their young. I also knew there were ways I could photograph animals to show the similarities and to express the deep feelings I hold for animals.

Upon seeing the wonderful beauty of mountain bluebirds, I knew I had found a way to share with others the most special of those inner feelings. Each of us can see the radiant colors and magic of these small birds. They make us smile in a way that touches a deep place in our hearts.

It is true that mountain bluebirds possess a magnificence all their own. Yet, there is also a special and very wonderful thing which happens after understanding that magnificence. That is, the way we see other animals takes on a new meaning. And it is my hope that my photographs are one way of allowing others to see the unique beauty of these other birds that share life in the forest or farms or mountains.

I would like to dedicate this book to my wife, Jean, my parents, and to Ron Hirschi. I would also like to thank Carl Sever, Mark Lukes, Linda Helm, Betty Lynskey, and Marguerite Cronin.
I am extremely grateful to all the people at Graphic-sha Publishing Co., Ltd., who worked on the publication of this book.

著者略歴
ギャレン・バレル
1952 アイオワ州マレンゴ近郊に生まれる
1974 コロラド州立大学で動物学の学位をとる
1977 ワシントン大学で動物学の学位をとる
1982 野生動物写真家として活動を開始する
1984 BBC写真コンテストで構図賞を受賞
作品集に "Headgear" "One Day on Pika's Peak" "City Geese" などが
ある。この他多数の作品が、アメリカ国内の自然科学関係の雑誌に
掲載されている。

ABOUT GALEN BURRELL

1952 Born on a farm near Marengo, Iowa
1974 Bachelor of Science degree in Wildlife Biology from Colorado State
University
1977 Master of Science degree in Wildlife Biology from University of
Washington
1982 Began his career as a wildlife photographer
1984 Won the Bristish Broadcasting Corporation's photo contest in the form
and composition division
1985 Founded OUR WILDLIFE publishing company
1986 *Headgear* (Dodd, Mead and Company, N.Y.)
One Day on Pika's Peak (Dodd, Mead and Company, N.Y.)
1987 *City Geese* (Dodd, Mead and Company, N.Y.)
Many other photographs have been published in natural history magazines
Office P.O. Box 2460, Poulsbo, Washington 98370 U.S.A.

青い鳥をさがして
In Search of MOUNTAIN BLUEBIRDS

Photographed by Galen Burrell ©

著　者　ギャレン・バレル
発　行　1987年4月25日　初版第1刷
発行者　久世利郎
発行所　株式会社グラフィック社
　　　　〒102　東京都千代田区九段北1-9-12
　　　　☎03-263-4318　FAX03-263-5297

印　刷　錦明印刷株式会社
製　本　錦明印刷株式会社
写　植　三和写真工芸株式会社

定　価　2,900円

ISBN4-7661-0427-7　C0072　¥2900E

本書に出てくる鳥の和名は、大学書林発行の
「世界鳥類和名辞典」(山階芳麿著)を参考に
しました。